PLATFORM PAPERS

QUARTERLY ESSAYS ON THE PERFORMING ARTS

No. 36
August 2013

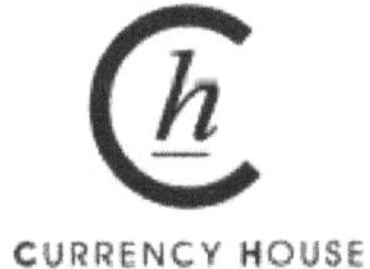

Re-Valuing the Artist in the New World Order

DAVID PLEDGER

PLATFORM PAPERS

Quarterly essays from Currency House Inc.

Founding Editor: Dr John Golder

Currency House Inc. is a non-profit association and resource centre advocating the role of the performing arts in public life by research, debate and publication.

Postal address: PO Box 2270, Strawberry Hills, NSW 2012, Australia

Email: info@currencyhouse.org.au Tel: (02) 9319 4953

Website: www.currencyhouse.org.au Fax: (02) 9319 3649

ISBN 978 0 9872114 5 3

ISSN 1449-583X

Typeset in 10.5 Arrus BT

Printed by Ligare Book Printers, Riverwood, NSW

Author's photo by D. Matvejevas

This edition of Platform Papers is supported by Katharine Brisbane, Janne Ryan, Larry Galbraith, Cathy Hunt, subscribers to Platform Papers and Friends of Currency House. To them and to all our supporters Currency House extends sincere gratitude.

Contents

1 RE-VALUING THE ARTIST IN THE NEW WORLD ORDER
DAVID PLEDGER

66 Readers' forum
Adam Cadell on *The Music of Place: Reclaiming the practice*, Platform Papers 35

AVAILABILITY *Platform Papers*, quarterly essays on the performing arts, is now published every February, May, August and November and is available by subscription, through your bookshop and on line. For an order form please visit www.currencyhouse.org.au

LETTERS Currency House invites readers to submit letters of 400–1,000 words in response to the essays. Letters should be emailed to the Editor at info@currencyhouse.org.au or posted to Currency House at PO Box 2270, Strawberry Hills, NSW 2012, Australia. To be considered for the next issue, the letters must be received by 15 September.

CURRENCY HOUSE For membership details, see our website at: www.currencyhouse.org.au

Acknowledgements

From Currency House, I am indebted to Katharine Brisbane who asked me to write something not knowing what she might get and Martin Portus for all his work in the background. The ideas for this paper have been some time in gestation and my conversations with, amongst others, Mary-Ann de Vlieg, Sandra Sdraulig and Nikos Papastergiadis have shaped my thinking considerably. I would also like to thank Eduardo Bonito for our late-night conversation a couple of years ago walking around the islands of Stockholm and to Catarina Saraiva for helping distil the facts from my memory of that chat. For reading and researching, my gratitude to Peter Eckersall and Kim Simpson. A special thanks also to Stuart Candy who knows me least of all but whose detailed consideration of a later draft assisted no end in delivering the final.

The author

DAVID PLEDGER is an intermedia artist working within and between the performing, visual and media arts. His work has been presented in theatres, galleries, museums, a car park, stables, a cattleyard, a suburban house, a film studio and at the Australian Institute of Sport. From his initial practice, live performance, he has developed an inter-disciplinary dramaturgy engaging with artists across art forms, and experts from social and academic fields. From 1995–2013 he was the founding director and producer of *not yet it's difficult*, one of Australia's leading interdisciplinary arts companies.

Performances include *The Austral/Asian Post-Cartoon: sports edition* (1997), *Scenes of the Beginning From The End* (2001), the multimedia plays, *K* (2002–5) and *Blowback* (2004), the opera *Cosmonaut* (2004), the dance-music laboratory *Ampersand* (2011–3); installation projects include *(not) the next-door neighbours* (2001), *Walk In Drive In* (with Callum Morton 2006), *The Meaning of Moorabbin* (2008), *Hoist* (2010), *He Took Us To the Cattleyard* (2012); film/digital projects include *The UnMaking Of* (1998), *Cosenza Vecchia* (2000), *Eavesdrop* (with Jeffrey Shaw, 2004), *urbanandsuburban* (2012).

A recipient of the Sidney Myer Performing Arts Award and the Kenneth Myer Performing Arts Medal for his work as director/designer and actor, David is a commissioned writer (SBS, Sydney Opera House, Playbox, Film Victoria) recognised by Victorian Premier's Literary Awards (*Blowback*, short-listed, Drama) and Australian Writers' Guild for New Media Writing (nomination, *Eavesdrop*). He has a Dip. Dramatic Art (Acting) NIDA, a BA (Politics, Cinema) and a MA (Asian Studies).

In Asia and Europe, David has worked with Suzuki Company of Toga (Japan 1990-1992), Moscow Centre for Research Into Human Movement (Russia, 1991); Iberia Films (Georgia, 1991); La Fabriks (France, 1991); Korean National University of Arts (Korea, 1994, 1997); International TeaterTreffen (Germany, 1995, 1999); Gekidan Kaitaisha (Japan 1999-2002); Centre for Media and Art (ZKM) (Germany, 2002); Seoul Performing Arts Festival (Korea, 2005, 2008); Liverpool Capital of Culture (England, 2005–7); Shanghai Dramatic Arts Centre (China, 2008); Instant Café Theatre (Malaysia, 2007–10); Hellerau (Germany, 2011).

As a cultural operator he works as an advocate for artists creating new spaces for them to operate in. He created and managed *R and D Cubed* (Arts Victoria, 1996–8) and initiated the *PAML Pilot Project* (DOCITA, 1998–9). He has served on consultative panels for City of Melbourne (Cultural Advisory Panel, 2000–2), Arts Victoria (Arts Leaders Reference Group, 1998–2000; Arts Innovation Chair, 2005–6). He was a delegate at the 2020 Summit (2008). From 2010–1 he lived in Brussels whilst establishing the IETM-Australia Council for the Arts Collaboration Project as its inaugural director.

Prologue

> *These days the largest corporation in the world protects its global assets under the guise of its talismanic brand 'Democracy'. Dull-eyed, slow-witted and obese, America P/L's ex-workers prowl the mid-West like zombies. Forever eastwards, a golden dawn is breaking where cashed-up middle classes burn money faster than they can make it, aware there will be no dawns, no twilights, no brightness without incineration of a different kind within two generations. Down South, the three continents compete for gold stars: Africa offers up bloody labor for the vampiric global middle class; South America continues its stubborn resistance to a long-lost, ideological war and Australia, an elite-squad of pond-swimmers trained to ignore all that goes on elsewhere in order to serve beer, wine and spirits to our Northern masters. This is the story of that Numbskull Nation.*

Artists deal in science fiction to sound warnings and inspire hope. We like to play with the notion that bending time can help us understand the conditions of our daily life and influence the future. The constructions are infinite. A possible future can throw light on the present. The past is a harbinger of the future. The present is the past's future. And so on...

In the scenario on the dust-jacket of our fictional airport novel, the future is already embedded in the present. Nations *have* become corporations. The largest corporation in the world *is* undergoing a takeover bid from the next largest corporation. And the ethics, dynamics and politics of the takeover are reflected in the degree to which the next tier of corporations is responding.

Enter Australia 2013. We are not the numbskull nation described. But nor are we the clever country that our marketing brochures proclaim. Inelegantly entwined with America P/L, only recently awakened to Asia and in denial of our status as a nation of islanders, Australia lies irritably halfway between her view of herself and reality. This liminal state plays havoc with our sense of identity and does nothing for our national self-confidence. It permeates our daily life more than we acknowledge, contributing a value-set that is more contradiction than complement. One day we are a sophisticated country adeptly wielding soft-power diplomacy; the next we kowtow to whichever country sits above us on the corporate ladder. So we live in curious times in which 'disconnection' is a key mode of being (operating, seeing).

None more so than for the Australian artist. Today, the best theatre is found in a place once upon a time and not so far away called Canberra; the best dance is on your television; the best art is on the street; the best music is in your ear and cinema is dead proclaimed so by Peter Greenaway ten years ago at the Berlin Film Festival. Economically, we artists are told that we are part of an industry. *But what kind of an industry is it, when as its primary producers, most of us live on or below the poverty line?* In the age of globalisation, artists are its canaries in the coalmine and we are struggling for breath. Which is a worry. Because if the artist is struggling to survive in a society as well-off as ours, what does it say about *our* future?

This state of affairs has much to do with a generational trend that has emerged in the democracies of America, Australia, the UK, and, more recently, in parts of Europe in which the value of the arts and artists has diminished. This trend is reflected in the ways in which the arts have a presence in civil society and in the behaviour of agencies responsible for creating and advocating that presence.

Whilst the manifestations are specific to nations and regions, there are underlying economic and political causes. These are largely due to changes in the mechanics of global capitalism. The key change is that, since the early 1990s conservative and post-socialist democracies have adopted a neo-liberal ideology that 'proposes government re-structure and re-scale social relations in accord with capitalism's unrestrained demands'.[1] The new values attendant to these changes have permeated the arts, in particular, and culture more broadly. The ramifications have been most deleterious for the artist whose influence, agency and income have been significantly eroded.

Understanding the conditions under which these circumstances have been created is the first step to re-valuing the arts in the twenty-first century. Our future lies in the way we understand, interpret, write and adapt this present tense. It is a matter for government, for the arts industry and especially artists. It asks us to think outside our prescribed domains and consider that the best way to re-value the arts in the new world order is to re-value the artist.

1

The current world order

As recently as five years ago, western and northern Europe comprised an impregnable cultural fortress. However, in 2010, cuts of varying degree were announced to the arts and culture budgets of some countries. Some of these (the smaller cuts) were perceived as necessary corrections and were largely embraced by the sector; others signalled the start of deep incursions into the financial viability of a previously-protected domain. Worst-hit was the Dutch cultural sector. The Dutch Government announced cuts to the arts and culture budgets of 25%.[2] By the time they were enforced in early 2013, twenty-four cultural and arts organisations were closed with the brunt of the cuts borne by the independent arts sector and international collaborations.[3] Across Europe a general state of perplexity spread, over the thinking, strategy and social dynamics behind the cuts. It challenged not just the EU but 'the idea of Europe'.

The introduction of national arts subsidies was integral to the Continent's response to the devastation of World War Two. Culture was the foundation on which shared identity, values, and relationships could be built among the peoples of Europe to ensure the preconditions of the two world wars would never recur.

To cut a national arts budget so drastically could only imply that the winds of commitment had changed. There was a real *Talking Heads* moment of: How did we get *here*?

Based in Brussels at the time,[4] I was asked my opinion as an outsider by an online arts journal.[5] Having undergone the conservative compression of the Howard years, my answer focussed not on the Netherlands' cultural dynamics but on the changing nature and behaviour of Capital in Western democratic societies and its impact on the cultural sector.

In traditional or conventional capitalism (we are talking Adam Smith, here) the cooperation of the workers was fundamental to its optimal functioning. In this model, the employer—the capitalist, the one making the profit—accepts that for Capitalism to be profitable the worker needs to be at least aspirationally if not concretely improving her lot.[6] Throughout the nineteenth and twentieth centuries, Capitalism moved from this idealised (and functioning) version, through an iteration in which power was concentrated in the State, towards the current version in which power is concentrated within the Corporation, a process that has essentially cannibalised the State, absorbing it into the corporate superstructure.

Some opine that this New Capitalism has its antecedents in fascist corporatism.[7] However, in the cradle of neo-liberalism, it is a more refined strain, a powerful mutation that breaks the contract between the employer and the worker because it is concerned with profit to the exclusion of the interests of labour. The worker is no longer central to the equation and has been replaced by the shareholder and consumer. The shareholder's concern is: 'How much profit can

I make?' The consumer's concern is: 'How much can I spend and on what?

The crippling problem for democracy is that not only has the shareholder/consumer supplanted the worker in the economic domain, they have replaced the citizen in the democratic domain. When previously the question 'How do we want to live?' was the basis of social interaction, the questions of profit and consumption now occupy the minds of the majority of individuals in Western democratic societies.

The displacement of the connection between worker and employer set off an ever-increasing chain of disconnections that has had serious ramifications for Western democracy and the global order. The shift in the mental space of the individual—from that of the citizen to that of the shareholder/consumer—fundamentally altered the prevailing set of values which balanced social, cultural, environmental and financial considerations to one dominated by the latter. In implementing the cuts, the Dutch demonstrate they are less interested in the questions of the citizen; they have turned away from the social-cultural contract—on which post-war European unity was based—towards self-economic interest. To use John Ralston Saul's terminology, *dis*interest has given way to *self*interest.

1. The Australian playground

In Europe, the displacement of the worker in the mind of the individual necessarily means the displacement of the artist. In Australia, where the artist and the worker have rarely been conflated, that displacement had a different shape. It did not push the artist *out* of the centre—we have never been there—but *further from* the centre. More than this, Australia's neo-liberal project generated its own peculiar set of preconditions that had negative impact on the social environment supporting the arts.

Throughout the late 1990s and early-mid 2000s, Prime Minister John Howard skilfully re-made Australia in his own image, or at least in an image he could regard and appreciate. He did this by a deft use of language and the tactic of 'wedge politics' which he turned into a political art form. He created untextured negative space in every debate by breaking the laws of acceptable speech and speech-making so that no one would understand what he said in order that we would all understand what he meant. It was a new language to maintain power in an Australia that was 'relaxed and comfortable'. This phrase in itself was repeated so often that its potency now stems from its repetition, not from its evident truth. It was a seductive mantra that insinuated its values into our view of ourselves. The problem was that the more we were told how relaxed and comfortable we were, the more edgy and ill-at-ease we became. The disconnect, between what we were told we were and how we felt, was palpable. It created a disabling effect within our social relations and our democratic aspirations, a strategy intrinsic to the neo-liberal political project.

Howard drew inspiration for his re-shaping of Australia from his American counterpart, George W. Bush, and the 'neo-con' cabal that stage-managed him. Bush compartmentalised moral values into 'good' and 'bad', and people into 'us' and 'them'. It was a simple strategy: relentlessly affirm difference until it becomes an inviolable truth. Like a bully in the playground, George W. Bush repeated ad infinitum: 'You're either with us or against us.' Within the space of months it evolved from a neologism to a self-perpetuating logic, to the point where Australia agreed to participate in a war and kill lots of people in a far-off country. The base logic follows that if we weren't 'with America' then we were 'against America'. Of itself, reason enough for them to come and kill us in *our* far-off country. A recent visitor to our shores, arch-conservative Dutch politician Geert Wilders uses this tactic to great effect:

> Wilders for instance has often used the catch phrase: 'This land is not intended to be...' over and over again. Without clarifying what that intention would be, who intended it or if there was any intention at all to begin with. What happens is that Wilders is using the same set of words over and over again, until it becomes a truth on its own.[8]

This is not just a clever rhetorical strategy, an art form of message-making; its aim is to eradicate complex thinking from public debate.

By using the discourse of the playground, Howard infantilised the Australian people, turning Australia into a country where the larrikin became a liability. As a nation, we became fearful and compliant. The 'fair dinkum, fair go' egalitarianism for which Australia was internationally renowned evaporated in a climate of anxiety. Our default setting switched from fun to fear: fear of difference, fear of change, fear of the shadows. Under Howard, Australians lost their mojo. And with that our embrace of risk, individuality and independence, critical values in the ecology of the arts and art-making.

Whilst artists tried to resist this 'ambient fear', institutions largely failed to support them. Self-censorship crept into the programming cultures of major organisations such as state theatre companies; festivals seemed reluctant to program poltically contentious Australian work. This new atmosphere created a 'Coalition of the Willing' approach to programming that we are yet to shake off.

2. Death by managerialism

In Western democracies, neo-liberalism is now the ascendant ideology. Ingested by government and business, neo-liberal values have permeated our public sector, leading to a radicalisation of its functions, objectives and values.

An important process in this has been 'the adoption of managerial practices that focus on issues of economic efficiency and increasing productivity in particular sectors'.[9]

The language here is important because of its reductive nature. Efficiency. Productivity. The umbrella term 'managerial practices' is a descriptor of behaviours and belief systems that equate with Managerialism, a way of looking at the world that has taken hold widely and aggressively within the arts, education and cultural sectors.

Managerialism is an ideology created by managers for managers. Its genesis lies in the thinking of expatriate Australian Elton Mayo, whose assessment of democracy as divisive and lacking in community spirit led him to look towards corporate managers to restore the social harmony that he believed immigration and industrialization had destroyed and democracy was incapable of repairing.[10] Managerialism is an alternative ideology to democracy, capitalism and communism. Twinned with neo-liberalism it is sometimes called New Managerialism. It may be described as:

> the set of knowledges and practices that inform neo-liberal operations and organisational governance.[11]

In the arts sector, managerialism has bred toxic strains. Partly because it had to adapt to the nature of the arts' core business, which is making art, an alchemical process which resists concretization. Managerialism sees itself as the antidote to chaos, irrationality, disorder, and incompleteness, essential elements in this alchemy.[12] More like a gas than a mineral, art is hard to contain, process and control. As soon as you think you have a handle on it, it morphs into something else. So arts agencies mutated various versions of managerialism to inhibit the arts' natural processes. For example, the Arts Council of England, long regarded as one of the more instrumentalist arts agencies, became ever more so, engaging the arts as an agent of social regeneration in the service of government (Blair 1998–2009); Creative Scotland recently moved to apply the language of the 'investment paradigm' to funding[13] (a creeping policy of Arts Victoria in its new Organisations Investment Program) and the Australia Council for the Arts (ACA) built a containment zone within the organisation from which art (and artists) could be observed and policy developed to 'manage' it (and them).

Whilst the ACA has bedfellows at state level, it is worthwhile digging a little deeper into the organisation's psychology: one, because it is the national arts body so my analysis can be afforded the greater scrutiny, and two, the ACA's situation is in flux because of the recent Australia Council Review and the subsequent recommendations contained in Creative Australia, the new National Cultural Policy. Debate is timely.

There is much to admire in the National Cultural Policy with regard to the Australia Council, however, it fails to penetrate the lower depths where independent artists live, a crucial remit of a national arts body. Nor does it deal with the behaviour of the ACA and its relationship to the artist and artistic practice in anything other than a generalist tone. The stated position of the artist's centrality to the nation and its future is not backed up with changes that put the artist at the centre of culture in anything other than a rhetorical sense: there is no commitment to changes to social security legislation enabling artists to continue to practise whilst out-of-contract; visual arists are not guaranteed fees for the exhibition of their work and there is no acknowledgement of policies that have diminished the artist's autonomy.

It is in Creative Australia's gaps where the independent artist remains subject to the managerialist reflex. To be fair, this is difficult to insinuate into a national cultural policy because its primary objective is the articulation of a national vision for culture. However, as focus shifts to the policy's implementation, it is necessary to assess the current state-of-play for artists and analyse the reasons why it is so and how it can change for the better.

3. The Australia Council for the Arts: A case study

Values. The consequences of Managerialism are felt profoundly where managers are professional managers as opposed to industry-specific managers. And it occurs *most* profoundly where the industry's primary workers are marginalised (in this case artists). This is where managerialism is both a medium of neo-liberalism and a function of it. Integral to its application is the transference of 'knowledge' or management practices across industry. It is why, for example, it is permissible for a former director of a telecommunications company to become the CEO of the national arts body.[14] According to managerialism, the skills required to run a telco department are the same as those required to run a national arts organisation. The methodology is the same regardless of an organisation's core business. The Australia Council's mission is to

> support the creation, presentation and appreciation of distinctive cultural works by providing assistance to Australian artists and making their works accessible to the public.[15]

Over the last decade, the efforts of senior management have concentrated on infrastructure and audience development largely because that was all it knew, having little understanding of art-making other than through the prisms of management, bureaucracy, communications and marketing, its recruitment base. This internal 'culture' insinuated a set of 'implicit values' sometimes called 'shadow values' which are communicated by and embody values that often run counter to the ACA's stated values of integrity, leadership, respect, collaboration, service and diversity.[16] This direction put it on a collision course with the professional arts field and government resulting in the 2012 Review.

From Service to Governance. In the managerialist paradigm, public services are governance structures geared to market efficiency,[17] Whilst this applies to the service organisation itself it is also projected onto the sector. In the small-to-medium arts sector, for example, the ACA's decision to use the Business Plan as an application model for funding Key Organisations privileged economic and administrative criteria over artistic merit and integrity. The oft-repeated mantra of arts tsar, Carrillo Gantner, fell victim to institutional amnesia long ago but bears remembering here: *'The arts should be business-like but they are not a business.'* Aside from the misguidedness of the ACA's approach, it was found that few, if any, ACA staff had sufficient experience in business to provide an appropriate level of constructive advice in the new paradigm. As artists, we felt they were in a constant process of upskilling due to a top-down directive; and that this led to their developing a protective risk-management approach which imposed further levels of compliance on applicants when providing advice of which they were uncertain. This process has done no one any favours. It runs counter to the social agency of the arts and leaves it vulnerable to the reductive processes of productivity and efficiency.

Unsurprisingly, the new governance values were communicated via a language and process that created an unproductive distance between the artist and the bureaucrat. This remains the case. The penetration of this langauge co-opted from the corporate sector has had bizarre manifestations in the small-to-medium sector. Companies employing no permanent full-time staff and/or a handful of part-timers are now headed up by a CEO (Chief Executive Officer). Often as not that position is now taken by a manager or administrator or producer, further displacing the artist. In some cases, where artists doggedly try to hold on to the power-spot in a company, they appropriate the corporate nomenclature. Where there is just an artist and one or two others in the office, 'The Artist as CEO' is beyond parody, a performative reality show where no one sees the joke. As the small arts company has become a new field in which to grow governance protocols, professional and artistic integrity are reduced to high farce and matters of art-making are relegated to incidental activity.

The obsession with infrastructure. The ACA's obsession with infrastructure has caused considerable damage to the arts ecology, in particular to the small-to-medium and independent sector. The argument that the infrastructure needs to be built before artists can be poured into it, is as wrong-headed as any ideologically-driven approach. Like wet cement, we will harden and concretize. In the meantime a whole generation of artists has been left to scavenge. Unsurprisingly, Australia's professional practising artist-population has decreased over the last ten years.[18] It is unlikely the same decline could be observed in the population of arts administrators (whether they be managers, producers, marketers, presenters or programmers).[19]

The idea that 'infrastructure' solves the problem of the artist's limited resources is fallacious. One reason is that governance structures come with conditions, often implicitly denoted, that suffocate and inhibit the artistic processes which they are supposed to support. Governance once meant guidance, not the disabling over-regulation that dominates the independent and small to medium sector. And if you are an artist that has not yet earned the privilege of playing this endgame then you are probably in the situation where, due to 'new initiatives', you are forced into foregoing production control to a new management structure that may lead to even less money ending up in your pocket. There is a one-size-fits-all approach to the independent and small-to-medium sector. The fact is these areas of artistic production are varied, complex and changeable. The lack of understanding of this matter within the ACA is astonishing.

The umbrella of diversity. In early 2012, the ACA introduced a structural reorganisation in which the Major Performing Arts Board (MPAB) organisations and the smaller Key Organisations were brought under the one umbrella. This move added to the widespread suspicion that the ACA views the small-to-medium sector as a feeder mechanism for the Majors. Such a re-structure ignored what the whole professional field knows: *that the small to medium sector is a separate ecology fulfilling a separate mission to those of the major organisations*. No one attending this year's National Theatre Forum could be left thinking any other way. The depth of conservatism in the major theatre companies is counterpointed by the sense of adventure in the small-to-medium and independent sector. Few of the dynamics of the small-to-medium sector have correlatives in the mainstream; few companies across the two sectors share the same artistic values, organisational design or professional aspirations. The strength of the performing arts is diversity, not homogeneity.

(Dis)respect. Compounding this view, and despite this evidence, is the fact that measurement tools such as Artistic Vibrancy, developed for the MPAB, have been passed on to the small-to-medium sector. This measurement reportedly arose from discussions with some MPAB board members who complained they had no shared language with their artistic directors. Senior management resolved to invent a new language. This was deemed to be so revelatory that it was passed on to Key Organisations in the small-medium sector, adding to the burden of KPIs required to fulfil their contractual obligations, and validating the spurious role industry gossip plays in assessment processes. As an ACA staff member explained to me, one measure of artistic vibrancy was that you were being talked about in theatre foyers. Aside from the sheer idiocy of this measurement, the anomalies are manifold, not the least of which is how MPABs have, in the first place, board members who cannot converse with their artistic directors and, in the second place, how artistic vibrancy can be a useful measure for a sector that behaves not at all like the Majors. Processes like these, based on ignorance, do nothing but engender disrespect for the artist and artistic practice. They support the notion that managerialist values have taken hold within the agency as they reflect the concentration of decision-making in a managerial paradigm as opposed to a cultural one.

The paradox of competition. The mantra that the arts must compete with other sectors in the social space is an imposition on the sector's growth. Whilst this may seem a paradox, it underlines the fact that the arts are first and foremost a public good. Competition reduces the arts to a commodity in a marketplace.

The dynamics of this contradiction is at the heart of the argument surrounding the value of the arts. *The ACA has failed to communicate and defend the arts as a public good, and chosen instead to sell it as cultural product.*

Internally, competition is an institutionalised mindset as art form departments have historically competed for the greatest share of the funding pie. This competitive mentality being projected onto the professional field forces another 'disconnect' as success in the field is actually based upon collaboration. Artists, companies, organisations and institutions rely on each other to cooperate in the creation, development and engagement of audiences for the kinds of work we produce. Until we reach some sense of critical mass in the mind of the public, the notion of competition within the arts remains destructive and counter-productive to its growth and relevance.

Fear of the individual. Further to this is the 'pogrommatic' approach to artists. In order to communicate, reflect, engage and lead, artists require a singularity of purpose, identity and practice: an active individualism from which they express themselves artistically. Managerialism specifically denies that the fundamental nature of society is an aggregation of individuals.[20] Unsurprisingly arts agencies have in recent times manifested an aversion to artists and in particular to artists operating independently.

In order to deal with artists—a key priority of any arts agency—the managerialist solution has been to turn the artist-individual into an artist-organisation, a first step to their institutionalisation. So artists have been encouraged to 'incorporate', to turn themselves into associations if not companies limited by guarantee. In this way the artist reflects an image that the arts agency can recognise and organise within its own mechanistic view of the world. For their part, the artist is introduced to the world of accountability and regulation, which, through sheer weight, sidelines their artistic practice and endeavour—a direct consequence and goal of managerialism as artistic expression is idiomatic to democracy.

Policy initiatives arose out of this need to control the artist. In Theatre, the decision to redirect presentation costs away from project funding to venues, deprived artists of their agency in dictating the direction of artistic and cultural production at a grass roots level. Where once it was possible for artists to use production grants to choose where they wished to produce a work and with whom, that responsibility now lies with programmers and producers.[21] For the independent theatre artist this has been a disaster. Now they must go cap in hand to gate keepers whose support is now vital in financing their project. Whereas they previously could have self-presented, now they are subject to curatorial discretion. Most recently an experienced, highly-regarded independent maker confided how they could no longer even hire a space in one of the main contemporary performing arts venues in their city because none of the creative producers considered their work sat within the curatorial aesthetic of the venue. One of the programs advertised as central to the Australia Council's new image is Cultural Leadership. This is a sick joke. *How can artists lead if they have no autonomy?*

Blinded by the bottom line. In the international policy of ACA there is a confluence of all these shadow values. Dominated by financial outcomes—the imperative to 'Sell! Sell! Sell!—there is barely a rudimentary understanding of the dynamics and values of international engagement in global culture. One does not engage internationally in the arts to make money. Ask any prominent European company with a substantial touring program and they will tell you that, at best, they break even. The reasons for engaging internationally are artistic curiosity, professional development and education, audience engagement, network-building and finding new partners for future collaboration. Income generation is a consequence of a sophisticated process. It is not the primary objective.

Finally it is in the international sector where all the worst aspects of the ACA's shadow values backfire because the organisation's market-based objectives for the arts have failed at the most fundamental level: to secure the biggest emerging market of the last 15 years, Asia. The failure of Australia's arts sector to maximise market potential there is abject. How can this be? Because the overriding values of the ACA's market-based approach marginalise the basic tenets of the arts as a public good and of culture as integral to national identity.

Understanding this equation is key to engaging with Asia. Most Asian societies

> tend to think of culture in vastly broader terms: culture is who you are and how you live; it is your history, language and philosophy; your family and your food; your heritage and collective aspirations… The arts exist to give tangible expression to this notion of who you are as a people…[22]

The obsession with the bottom line in matters of the arts and culture is treated with suspicion in Asian contexts, and whilst in the past we have gotten away with this complacency, nowadays the shift in the balance-of-power to Asia exposes us for the aggressive nation-state marketers we are. The big problem for the Australia Council is that it has almost zero cultural literacy of Asia. In a time when it should have grown a staff base with genuine long-term experience and knowledge of Asia, its focus on so-called 'market objectives' played it out of the main cultural game there. To be clear, its recent repositioning of Asia in its international strategy did not come from any internal correction but from pressure through the office of ex-Arts Minister Simon Crean. The ACA's ignorance of Asia and its arrogance towards Australia's value to Asia has done the sector a real disservice, disarming us of the significant advantage provided by geographic proximity and geo-political empathy.

The impact on the artist and their work

For an artist, it is essential to consider the effects of managerialism on how and what they produce. Much of what I have referred to reflects the industrial conditions of the independent artist. This is the reality: producers spend most of their time producing, managers managing and marketers marketing; artists spend disproportionately more time writing applications for funding their work than they do on making it. The process is a debilitating one. It is unsurprising that these circumstances eventually detract from the work itself.

It is difficult to discern from the inside what these deficits are, how they manifest in the process and the work that is made. To garner an objective point of view I have been thinking a lot of the discussions I had when based in Brussels. After spending much of my time in discussion with European cultural operators, it was clear there was considerably less enthusiasm for Australian work than there used to be. In translating their many observations, the best way to describe their criticism is that Australian work can exhibit a tendency to be over-managed.

What does this mean? In the first place, it means that considerably more financial resources and thinking are put into managing, marketing and producing an artistic work than in making it. Before an idea is allowed to grow, to see whether or not it has genuine potential, it is marketed, managed and produced within an inch of its life, and this unproductive alchemy is integrated and perceived in the work. This is not about Australian work being better or worse than European work but about it being less vital than it used to be because of the structures under which it is now made. This is directly linked to Council's focus on the kind of infrastructure that devolves artistic practice to a marginal activity, a focus that privileges output and income over artistic quality, process and cultural agency.

It also places the artist in a contorted position. Generally speaking, Australian artists seem to have developed the habit of looking at what is immediately in front of them rather than what is on the horizon. This is very much a managerialist reflex. We have become overly careful not to fall, in case we are crushed by the whole house of cards now resting prematurely on our shoulders. Artists elsewhere, in many parts of Europe particularly, tend to focus on what is ahead of them. It is the reason why so much international work presented in Australia is sourced from Europe. Artistic quality increases considerably when it is created in an environment that is not risk-averse and in which the artistic impulse is not overloaded with expectations before its true value can be assessed. These are familiar concerns expressed by Australian artists and producers disturbed by the conditions in which they create and produce.

The concentration of managers in the decision-making apparatus of the ACA is also troubling. In preparing for this paper I invited arts professionals to assess the proportion of artist representation on the Australia Council's art form boards to which they were most closely aligned.[23] The survey produced a surprisingly varied snapshot. The Visual Arts and Music boards have six of seven members who identify as artists. The Dance and Theatre boards each with seven members, have, respectively, two and one. In very few of these instances are the artists independent—that is, not formally attached to an institution such as a company or a university. One can argue that by denying an appropriate level of artist representation, the Dance and Theatre Boards are and have been operating in breach of the Council's mission. It begs the question: *How can the ACA advocate for the value of the artist in society when it does not value the artist itself?*

This is a serious conundrum not just for the agency but the industry at large. It is a marker of a deeper problem in Australia's artistic and cultural production sector. In terms of influence, income and agency, artists are at the bottom of the food chain: they sit below the funding, management, governance and producing structures and yet they are the only essential element in the equation. Theirs is the only activity which, if taken away, would collapse the industry. In much of Europe there is a level playing field across the arts profession and there is an implicit if not tacit understanding and acknowledgment that without the artist no one would have a job. This appreciation is often reflected in their employment conditions particularly in Western and Northern Europe. If one is to seriously apply an industrial model to cultural production in Australia, the question in the introduction needs to be reiterated: *How can there be an arts industry when the primary producer, the artist, has no guaranteed income, and in the majority, lives below the poverty line?*

4. Creative Australia: Putting the arts back into the Australia Council

The preceding sections summarise an artist's impression of the daily life conditions of the independent artist framed by current Australia Council attitudes, behaviours and policy initiatives. If you were to take the points of view of any number of arts professionals, different stories would be told, much of it critical of our national arts body. As we now know, such stories came to light in submissions to the National Cultural Policy to the extent that an independent review was deemed essential. This led to the decision to enable legislation to be enacted to bring about structural change within the organisation.

The main argument for the new legislation is that the grammar and vocabulary of contemporary arts practice has fundamentally altered over the last twenty years and the agency's governing parameters need to be brought up-to-date. This is now an accepted view. The new legislation will bring about a disarticulation of the art form boards. In the matter of grants allocation, a new model is to be implemented that replaces the standing Art Form Board structure with a general stream for grant applications across all art forms.[24] This could do a number of things: eradicate the internal competition for Council funds which puts departments in adversarial relationships; put an end to the erratic and sporadic cross-art-form initiatives that have become the spakfilla holding up a dilapidated policy house, and end the misery of the Inter-Arts Office which has carried the unrealistic expectations of being the panacea for the agency's failure to embrace the twenty-first century. However, as with any legislation, its effectiveness is in the implementation. The exercise will be pointless if the structural elements of the organisation are simply re-named. Changes in the law need to be reflected in *fundamental* changes in the organisation's design in line with a renewed commitment to its stated values.

Changes. First we need to rethink how those values are insinuated into the fibre of the organisation so that its attitudes, practices and policy no longer reflect the shadow values that currently hold sway. These shadow values view the artist as a singular, competitive entity producing a cultural product for which it deserves neither respect nor pay. In its new incarnation, the Australia Council needs to be *for the arts*—not for arts management, not for arts marketing and not for the agency itself. The renewed commitment should be based on the Australia Council's mission—'to support the creation, presentation and appreciation of distinctive cultural works by providing assistance to Australian artists and making their works accessible to the public'. *In the context of the current state of play this means the arts ecology must be re-imagined so that artists sit with and not beneath the other agents in artistic and cultural production.*

Key to this is building an understanding that infrastructures are created in response to the artistic process not vice-versa. Changes to the legislation governing the ACA will be meaningless if it fails to understand the various ways in which artists work and the responsive, flexible, varied and unique structures required to enable them to do so. At this juncture, the small-to-medium and independent arts ecology is infrastructure-heavy, ideas-light, inflexible, under-resourced and counter-intuitive. *Only in an environment in which the forms of artistic and cultural production are defined by the artists and their practice can the arts genuinely flow and grow.*

As it is. In terms of income, influence and agency, the artist's lot is a parlous one. Direct funding for individual artists in Australia has fallen by about one-third since the 1990s.[25] In real terms, they earn less from their artistic practice than they did twenty years ago.[26] They are barely visible at elite levels of governance and advice. Their numbers are decreasing. Their autonomy has been compromised and curtailed by policy that has institutionalised them within organisations, venues and programs. It is not fair to slate home to the ACA alone the blame for this state of affairs, although it has been its main progenitor. In truth, the diminution of the artist has been facilitated within and by the Australian arts industry whose growth is directly linked to maintaining the artist's inequitable position in the current world order.

2

The new world order

The argument outlined above is that the working conditions of the artist today are directly related to ideological change driven by economic imperatives on the global stage. Neo-liberalism and managerialism are the dominant ideologies determining these conditions. At present, we are in their thrall. In the future, the world will open up. The era of the world dominated by the white, English-speaking peoples is coming to a close and with it the absolutism attached to a single dominant agent. China, Brazil and India provide different and contesting models of human agency in the twenty-first century. In its second half, Africa will re-shape what they make of it. Diversity, pluralism and difference in language, culture and race are the rough interface of globalisation. It is also where contemporary artistic practice resides. As these 'edges' interplay and begin to comprise a new centre, a new world order, artists will be integral to making sense of this changing global landscape because the characteristics of the 'new' will come from where they live and operate, the periphery, the edges of society. *If you want to know where you will be in twenty years, follow an artist. If you want to get there before everyone else, fund them.*

The other key notion here is that of 'interconnectedness' and the role artists play by bringing together culture, race, artistic practice and social issues. In this they are adhesive, they are the glue that sticks these elements together and shapes them, talks about them, constructs them in as many ways as there are people trying to relate to them. In artistic language this is called 'process', or if you are from the theatre, dramaturgy—the process of connecting and matting ideas into practice. In a broader application 'dramaturgy' is an adaptive notion that embraces the idea of an operating system whether that be of a production or culture. At its core is the element of change. Applied in this way the notion of an artistic dramaturgy as the operating system of the twenty-first century is a compelling one.

The world is in a state of high flux brought about by technological and ecological evolution. On all indicators it is expanding, and operating systems that behave otherwise, such as economic and ideological systems, will become anachronisms because of their intrinsic reductive nature. Most changes in the world—environmental, political, social and economic—can be explained by the playing out of the tension between reduction and expansion, the push-and-pull of globalisation. Artists sense and articulate this tension because they work at the edge of things, they feel the shifts and changes, they internalise and express them, they mediate upheaval and explain crisis, they 'see' issues of social and mental well-being as intrinsic to their artistic practice, they see into the spaces between things and the languages they use are not bound by words so they have a capacity to speak to everyone. For artists, feeling is a vocational tool, they are society's antennae, the canaries in the coalmine of global change. The intuitive process of the artist and their ability to engage with and facilitate process, change, experiment and discovery are the assets of our time. In the new world order, the artist will be at its centre. *We are the key sensors and connectors in the twenty-first century and nations and societies that understand this will be more culturally, socially, environmentally and economically viable.*

How do we get to this future in Australia?

To begin with, we need to extend ourselves and our reference points. There are as many ways of valuing, structuring and organising artistic and cultural endeavour as there are countries in the world. Historically Australia has stuck with the Anglo-American paradigm, the reliance on which has for years set back genuine progress in our policy development. Our default setting has been to see ourselves through this duality without acknowledging our wider cultural heritage, geographical proximity and unique characteristics. As the artist Juan Davila asked of us thirty years ago: *'We should find a dialogue constituting ourselves as a difference, not as a peripheral "another", but as a sustained contradiction.'*[27]

To wit, I would like to draw down information from Asia and Europe, the two halves of the geo-cultural axis that will define Australia's future in the first quarter of this century. Asia and Europe are linked in the Australian imaginary by geographical proximity in the first place and cultural empathy in the second. Conscious of the value of exploring the fraternity of the southern hemisphere, I will also cite trends in Brazil.

We're going to these places to collect information on how culture, the arts and artists, are valued elsewhere. How do other nations value the agency of culture within their societies? How and why do they value the arts and artists? This process will help us appreciate and understand key issues of regional, national and international context, our own uniqueness and the role of temporality which will assist in mapping a cultural topography on which Australia can base future policy settings in the context of Creative Australia and the new world order. It will help us build a bridge between our present and our best future.

1. The agency of culture

The idea that Asia is not one country is just starting to take hold in Australia. For decades our foreign policy lived in the shadow of White Australia. White Australia could just as easily have been called One Asia for all the insights it brought to the cultural, ethnic and racial tapestry that confounds definition of the Asian continent. In 2012, Australia's acknowledgment of Asia was somewhat rehabilitated by the *Australia in the Asian Century* white paper. Recent significant bilateral arrangements with Indonesia, India and China have brought us back to a future imagined by Whitlam and Keating in which Australia's and Asia's future were inextricably linked. Unfortunately, any allusions to the role of culture in these new arrangements are desultory. Even more so given a timely Platform Paper by Alison Carroll and Carrillo Gantner that argued strongly for culture to be in the vanguard of our engagement there,[28] an approach some Asian nations have productively refined.

The value of cultural agency in international engagement is high in East Asian countries like Singapore, Japan and Hong Kong. Further south, the biggest impression could still be made by Indonesia. However, it is the success of the cultural program of the

Republic of Korea (Korea) over the last twenty years that provides compelling instruction for Australia.

Korea. Korea punches at around the same weight as Australia in terms of its potential to wield soft power through culture. Its trajectory often intersects and competes with Australia's. Korea is a regional neighbour and a featured protagonist in our twenty-first century Asian narrative. There are, of course, fundamental and idiosyncratic differences between Korea and Australia in history, geography, evolution of political culture and cultural politics but a brief analysis of the how and why of Korea's achievements can reveal useful information, especially in the story of a country that understands the value of its national identity, and the centrality of the arts in defining and communicating it.

I first worked in South Korea in 1993, one year after a civilian was elected President for the first time in forty years. In those days countries were classified as first, second or third world. Against most indicators South Korea was a second world country struggling in the aftermath of a 30-year cycle of invasion, occupation and dictatorship. Pop star PSY's suburb, Gangnam, was an ephemera, a dream way beyond household income thresholds that barely registered on the OECD gazette. Today, Korea is a regional powerhouse. How did it transform itself in one generation?

Hallyu. From the late 1990s, the 'Korean Wave' or Hallyu washed up on the shores of neighbouring countries. Artist and artisan-led, Korean TV soaps, magazines, films, fashion, music and performing arts made a phenomenal impact, exceeding the expectations of a population of fifty million umbilically cut from its northern half and vulnerable to the volatile geopolitics of the region. Even China was smitten. On the back of this wave, Korea turned itself inside-out from a country beset by a crippling identity crisis to a nation hell-bent on internationalizing itself from the ground up.

Two main factors accelerated this movement: the success of Korea's co-hosting with Japan of the 2002 World Cup and a shift in the nation's political dynamics towards an active appreciation of the value of culture in the process of internationalisation.

World Cup 2002. Dutchman Guus Hiddink is a national hero in Korea. As coach of the Korean soccer team, Hiddink took the country into the 2002 World Cup semi-finals, one better than its co-host, Japan. Whilst the argument that a nation's sporting success is directly linked to a nation's positive identity is anathema to much of the Australian performing arts community, it doesn't play that way in Korea. On the day of the semi-final, friends expressed wonderment at the feeling on the streets in Seoul where a reported ten million Koreans stepped out to celebrate going past their old rival in anticipation of greater glory. Old and young, usually separated by tradition and custom, joined hands as one, the latter dressed in costumes made from cut-ups of the Korean flag, an action previously deemed a treasonable offence. The problems of inter-generationalism were submerged that night and never resurfaced with the same potency. More importantly, Korea's chip on its shoulder with Japan—fueled by the latter's brutal occupation of the peninsula in mid-twentieth century—evaporated in the blink of a penalty shot. Around the same time as Australians lost their mojo, Koreans found theirs.

We are Korean. The second factor played out very publicly in the global economy. Sent bankrupt by the 1997 Asian economic meltdown—or, if you are Asian, the IMF crisis—the Korean federal government artfully restructured the nation's financial frameworks so that within a decade it had resumed its role as the world's fastest-growing economy.[29] One of its strategies was to place the arts at the vanguard of its policy because Korea's political culture understood that for its economic motivations to be understood, the basic Korean character and sensibility needed to be explained, communicated and appreciated. And so it strategically funded the cultural sector—regionally, by instigating an atmosphere of productive competition; nationally, by promoting Korean culture to a growing domestic audience and internationally, by committing funds to new policy, international collaborations and touring. Significant initiatives underpinning this strategy are the exhibition quotas on Korean and foreign films which enabled the domestic viability and international success of the Korean film industry; the establishment of the Korean National University of Arts which has brought new levels of excellence and expertise into the professional arts community and the ambitious Asian Culture Hub City in Kwangju, a new concept in urban design linking artistic thinking and practice to local and regional questions of Asian identity.[30]

The key driver of this development is indeed identity, or more precisely—and invoking the advice of Juan Davila—the need to understand and communicate the value of one's own identifying parts so as to distinguish oneself from others. In Korea's case this is borne out of their survival of occupations by Japan and America. In very different ways both occupations threatened their language and culture but instilled a sense of purpose at all levels of society. Political and cultural resistance eventually prevailed and became manifest in Korea's current global agency. Meanwhile the ever-present elephant in the room—the separation from the North—bears down on this analysis. It is impossible to know what role it plays in this equation other than to say that if occupation inspires resistance then separation conjures grief, and to conquer grief, a new life must be made, a new identity forged. Korea has appreciated the central role of the arts in shaping its cultural identity, and the value of the artist as mediator, communicator, interpreter, a secular shaman in the modern incarnation of this uniquely conflicted country.

Flanders. Flanders, Walloonia and a small German-speaking community constitute the Federal State of Belgium in Western Europe. They represent three distinct communities and language groups although the last is so small official population breakdowns usually put figures at Flemish (60%) and Walloon (40%).

Over the last twenty years the Flemish have led a renaissance in Western European contemporary performance which has had far-reaching global influence. Part of the reason is the calibre of artists like Anna Teresea de Keersmaker (Rosas), Alain Platel (C de la B), Josse de Pauw (Victoria/CAMPO), Jan Fabre (Troubleyn) and cultural operators such as Hugo van Greef, Ann Olaerts, Guy Gypens, Guido Minne and Frie Leysen. Together they have created an alternative ecology so profoundly successful that the mainstream threw their arms in the air and decamped to quieter pastures. The other part of the reason is that, like Korea, Flanders was driven by a desire to 'exceptionalise' its culture, to produce a contemporary Flemish identity in which their performing arts and fashion were central and distinctive. That's all very well, of course. At various times, many cultures had and have these two quixotic ingredients. What the Flemish did was create an entity that would help stick the lot together.

The Flemish Theatre Institute (VTI) formed in 1987, became a signifcant agent of cultural renovation and rehabilitation. For the Flemish contemporary arts, VTI advocates for it, explains it, articulates it to government and in some cases back to the sector and itself. It is part broker, part advocate, part policy maker, part trendsetter and educator. It has grown naturally out of a set of real needs: it balances argument for cultural growth with social and financial awareness. The Institute folds ideas and processes back on themselves developing a *raison d'être* shaped rather like an undulating matrix—networked and curvilinear. They explain their process very well:

> Applied research is a major component of VTI's work because it converts the information in the database and collections into a useful form. The research is applied to actual practices by means of descriptive and analytical fieldwork. In this regard, the performing arts are not simply the object of research, but also play an active part in shaping opinion.[31]

The intellectual capital grown by VTI has helped the Flemish contemporary performance scene respond and adapt to local and European trends and eventually lead them. The make-up and operation of companies, such as C de la B and CAMPO in Ghent and Toneelhuis in Antwerp, speak to an artistic curiosity that collapses the boundaries of discrete art form practice and hierarchical models of artistic direction. The strength of these organisations lies in their ability to adapt their structures and production modes to artists' needs and their interests in the world. It is here that the word 'contemporary' has its true meaning.

Australia. Australia needs a think-tank that cuts transversally through society providing feedback to the cultural sector and a provocation to its *raison d'être*, an inter-disciplinary and cross-portfolio mediator with long tentacles that can reach into all sectors, mine for critical data and come up with an appraisal that simultaneously challenges established thinking and provokes new thought on how the arts and culture interrelate in and with the rest of society. VTI is an excellent model.

Even greater value may be found in Korea's story. It is a narrative of resistance in the face of adversity. If that is an element required to shape a nation's identity, where do we find it in our own story? Australia is still the Lucky Country. We are one of the world's largest economies, ranked twelfth for our GDP,[32] which has recorded sustained growth since the mid-1970s.[33] Our cities are some of the most liveable in the world.[34] But a nation's story depends on who is telling it, and which events are privileged over others. Migrant stories are the stuff of legend in Australia and there is plenty of instruction to be found there. However, Australia's great story of adversity and resistance belongs to our indigenous people. Their activism is the bedrock of our cultural activism. Indigenous Australia's cultural warriors have fought valiantly, intelligently and progressively over the last two generations in particular, creating a momentum that continues today. There are lessons to be learnt here by Australia's non-indigenous cultural operators: strategy, determination, resilience, lateral thinking and clear communication that culture is the key to identity, and that the agency of culture in a society is a reflection of its maturity. To go even further, if the notion of an artistic dramaturgy as the operating system of the twenty-first century takes hold, Australia's indigenous culture offers the contemporary world valuable instruction in understanding the depths of interconnectedness as a foundation for living, perceiving and being.

2. The value of the arts

Brazil. In Brazil right now there are three interesting facts that reflect the value placed on arts and culture in Brazilian society. They operate within the broader framework of the arts-and-culture scene in Brazil which is very different from ours. One point of difference is useful to consider. Australia's cultural landscape is sometimes described as a field of silos, isolated and separated by distance. Brazil is multi-layered, an interweaving of variations on the theme of identity. In Brazil, 'there are many Brazils'.[35]

1: The arts are a public good. In Rio de Janeiro, the new Secretary of Culture recently divided the funding pool evenly into two sectors—not-for-profit and commercial. Whereas the commercial sector's funding is treated as an investment, the not-for-profit sector's funding is an unconditional grant. This is driven by a philosophical imperative that the arts are a public good and should not bear the expectation of realising profit.

The coda is that the arts be accessible to everyone.

2: Culture is a rhizome. During the 1970s, philosophers Gilles Deleuze and Felix Guattari developed the idea of the rhizome as a model for society and culture. The rhizome is an endless entity without beginning, characterized by *'ceaselessly established connections between semiotic chains, organizations of power, and circumstances relative to the arts, sciences, and social struggles.'*[36] Brazil's 4,000 Culture Points Program seems a fair imagining of this model. A Culture Point is located within an organisation, company or group that specialises in activities across a broad spectrum from the presentation of professional art works to arts training or the development of folk arts. In this non-hierarchical context, each organisation receives 23,000 Euro annually from the National Ministry of Culture to implement programs that talk about and create culture locally. On an annual basis all Points interact at a national convention then return to their respective nodes. In a rhizomatic model, growth and productivity are mediated within a continuum.

3: Access to culture is food for the soul. In 2013, the Brazilian Government will give to workers a 'Culture Stipend' of $25 a month for cultural expenses paid for by an electronic card that limits spending to cultural goods. These can be anything from books, DVDs, tickets to theatre, concerts, to movies and exhibitions. In keeping with Brazil's direct tax incentives for contributions to cultural groups and activities, 90% of the stipend will be covered by employers who can claim it on their income tax and workers pay the difference. Announcing the new incentive, Culture Minister Marta Suplicy said: *'Now we are creating food for the soul;*

Why should the poor not be able to access culture?'[37] Left to employers to decide whether to extend the benefit to workers earning up to five times the minimum wage, there is the prospect of injecting $3.5 billion into the cultural sector. The process operates in a similar way to a tax credit for household spending, and is not unlike an ongoing stimulus package for the arts.

Germany. Germany is a culturally confident nation. Its international agency, the Goethe Institute, communicates this confidence to all parts of the globe. Described as 'the Federal Republic of Germany's cultural institution operational worldwide', the Goethe Institute's three principal objectives are to promote the study of the German language abroad, to encourage international cultural cooperation and to convey an all-round image of Germany by providing information on its culture, society and politics. The language here is quite prosaic and the objectives compare with those of other nations' international agencies like Institut Français, Pro Helvetia, the Canada Council for the Arts and the British Council. What distinguishes the Goethe Institute is its capacity to understand the value of the arts in an altruistic context.

> We, the staff around the world, represent an open Germany. We build bridges that cross cultural and political borders. The fact that people speak openly with one another and work together in a visionary way enables something brand new and exceptional to be generated from our work. We develop the skills to question our self image as well as the perception of others and deal with cultural diversity constructively. We open doors between the arts, education, science and development and we trust

> in the power of art and its ability to ask questions and unsettle. We search for answers to the future questions of a globalised world.[38]

The language here reflects a deep understanding and appreciation of the value of the arts. Art is privileged for 'its ability to ask questions and unsettle' by an organisation established to 'build bridges that cross cultural and political borders' that represents one of the largest democracies in the world to the rest of the world. In Germany the arts are key to national identity and are recognised as key to the identities of all nations—a leap not always made by others. It is based on placing oneself in a position of both instruction and learning, a key mode of cultural exchange.[39]

The extent to which the Goethe Institute applies these values and practices to policy is most obvious in Asia, where it has created untold goodwill for Germany through established programs of cultural engagement with developing Asian countries that are independent of core German participation. Theirs is a sophisticated response to fast-changing regional dynamics and an acknowledgement of the power of art to transform and inform economic, political and social agendas. At its foundation is a willingness to advocate for the intrinsic importance of the arts.

Australia. In Australia any idea that the arts are a public good has been eroded by the popular index that reduces art to an economic unit of cultural consumption, a commodity. The arts industry has been a party to the application of this value-measurement both as a nod to the aggressive creative industries push and as an accepted value that has taken hold within the industry. Output and income are the key performance indicators required to justify funding; quality and process are secondary. Remarkably, a culture like Brazil's that privileges art above commerce stands to reap the greater economic benefit.

Australia does not yet have the capacity of Germany to embrace the high value of culture and the arts to our own society let alone a global society. Fair enough. Many nations fail to achieve this level of maturity. But theirs is an approach that has much instruction. It is no coincidence that Germany's economic, social and environmental indices are some of the highest in Europe. Further, the altruistic values that Germany assigns to the arts are directly connected to the belief that the arts are a public good and the role of the artist in society is central to national identity. These are natural stepping-stones.

Because we are starting from a low base, a key to increasing the value of the arts in the wider social domain is advocacy. This may take the form of individual advocacy, organisational advocacy or advocacy by a network. Two European networks provide useful references for determining a mission and an operational form.

Culture Action Europe, formerly, the European Forum for the Arts and Heritage, is a broad EU level platform for arts advocacy founded in the early 1990s. It was rebranded in 2008 as Europe's political platform for arts and culture. Its aim is to influence European policies for more and better access to arts and culture across the Continent and beyond. Founded by cultural operators and associations, the platform is characterised by its openness and effectiveness. It provides customized information and analysis on the European Union, and offers cultural actors a space to exchange and elaborate common positions and develop advocacy actions towards European policymakers. It is currently running a highly visible campaign called We Are More which mobilises those who care about the arts and culture in Europe to influence the EU's political negotiations for the 2014–20 EU Culture Program Budget.[40] It has good form with this kind of imaginative agitation: the 70 Cents for Culture Campaign directly contributed to the doubling of European citizens' contribution to the 2007–13 Budget.

Industry legend has it that A Soul For Europe was conceived at the turn of the century by a bunch of highly influential, mostly German and Dutch cultural operators and retired politicians who sat down to dinner together, opened up their address books, realised they knew half the leaders of Europe and asked why they were not exploiting this access to power. True or not, in 2004, A Soul For Europe was created: a mechanism by which influential culture folk could lobby their agendas in the corridors of EU power. Their agenda became the organisation's mission: to activate civil society to play a bigger role in creating Europe, and to use culture as the basis of their engagement.[41] The reasons for the mission are manifold. Firstly, in the 1990s, when culture was proclaimed a no-go zone for EU policy by many national governments, cultural operators had to come up with new ways of insinuating culture into the EU matrix. Secondly, and this is a somewhat more recent development, is the growing sense that Europeans see themselves as European as well as national citizens—certainly true of the younger generation, many of whom are graduates of the cross-Europe education program, Erasmus—and that this identity is directly linked to the building of European culture.[42]

Whereas Culture Action Europe is the primary arts and culture lobby in Europe, A Soul For Europe tries to get citizens interested in a Europe of cultures. Both identify as bottom-up initiatives. Focussing the lessons of these two networks through the prism of the Flemish Theatre Institute and blending them with local variations such as the National Association of the Visual Arts (NAVA) and Theatre Network Victoria (TNV) could be a first step to establishing a genuine arts-advocacy platform in Australia.

3. The value of the artist

Belgium and France. In some Northern and Western European countries, artists receive stipends of varying amounts and for varying periods. In Denmark, for instance, 275 artists are granted an annual stipend of between 15,000 (AUD$2,500) and 149,000 Danish Krone (AUD$25,000) every year for the rest of their lives.[43] Ireland still offers generous tax exemptions to artists on income up to 40,000 Euros, although since 2011 exemptions come with more stringent qualifications. Further south, Belgium and France offer different but compelling versions of artist's benefits.

In Belgium, for example, there is the 'artist's statute' of around 1,000 Euros a month. To obtain it, the artist must prove paid employment for 312 days over an 18-month period or 16,000 Euros in income derived from professional arts practice over the same period.In France, a similar system has existed in various guises since the 1930s. Under the title *intermittent du spectacle* the artist must prove 507 hours of paid employment over a ten-and-a-half month period. These kinds of systems appreciate the seasonality and financial insecurity of the artist's life and the essential value of the artist in the equation of artistic and cultural production. In both Belgium and France, generous direct subsidy programs known as *subvention* also exist enabling artists not only to survive but also to create new work. This combination has enabled the arts and cultural sectors of both countries to be regional and international powerhouses.

Given the lean economic times Europe is experiencing, the French system has come under scrutiny amidst threats to cut or reduce it. Out of this conflict a number of strong arguments for its maintenance have emerged. One is that without the *intermittent du spectacle* system, economic circumstances would further deteriorate. French arts economist Françoise Benhamou confirms its significance to the cultural economy: *'The entire economic equilibrium of the audio-visual world and theatre is based on it.'*[44] In practice, employment within some small theatre companies is grounded in paying the obligatory 507 hours a year knowing that the system will pick up payment for the rest via the benefit. It is on this basis that the independent French sector functions well and has garnered national and international currency. The importance of the system to artists, the cultural sector and society in general cannot be underestimated. In 2003 when plans were afoot to scrap the system, striking arts workers closed the Avignon Festival, threatened closure of the Cannes Film Festival and brought about the departure of the then Culture Minister.

Australia. On the island below this island-continent is the Museum of Old and New Art (MONA). Made by David Walsh in Hobart, MONA is not just any museum but quite possibly the most adventurous, provocative, synthesised contemporary arts museum in the world. Architecture, artistic intent, curatorial rigour are all in harmony. As an exemplar of the philanthropic model it is multi-faceted and subversive. Artists are drawn to it but not for these reasons alone.

Firstly, MONA is an art work itself and the art works it houses are connected to that which houses them, architecturally, artistically, spiritually. Artists feel they are in the presence of other artists in a house conceived and built by an artist (or at least someone for whom the artistic impulse is integral to their conception of the world). More importantly, embodied in the enterprise is a profound understanding that the key relationship in the arts is between the artist and the audience. All else pivots on this.

Secondly MONA reminds artists what they have lost. The Museum and its festival offshoots—MOFO and Dark MOFO—are comparatively corporate-light spaces. This is in marked contradiction to the major Festivals. The weight of sponsors, the emphasis on branding, the interplay of corporate governance in the programming, all these create an environment which reflects and iterates the role the arts play as an excuse for advertising portals. Given the spirit of artistic adventure and curiosity that inspired the birth of Australia's international arts festivals, it is perverse that these days they affirm most palpably the diminution of the artist as, for the first time ever, no artist leads a major Australian festival.

Finally, MONA imbues the spirit of genuine artistic agency: it embraces risk. In Richard Flanagan's recent article on David Walsh, he refers to Walsh's compulsion.

> Walsh frequently refers to a passage of Dostoevsky's that he says perfectly captures the gambling soul. 'I wanted to astonish the spectators by taking senseless chances' Dostoevsky wrote in *The Gambler*, 'and—a strange sensation!—I clearly remember that even without any promptings of vanity I really was suddenly overcome by a terrible craving for risk.'[45]

And so it is for the artist.

If there is one value that needs to be uplifted across the arts sector in Australia, it is risk. Risk-taking is key to a vital arts ecology. MONA embodies the anxiety that comes with great risk and the palpable excitement of creating something genuinely new, something that all artists aspire to. In its very particular circumstance, MONA values the artist as an independent, as a risk-taker and as a social agent whose value increases the closer they are to their audience.

To behave like this, we need to survive financially. In Belgium and France, financial value is a corollary of the artist's perceived social and cultural value. In Australia, our social, cultural (and economic) agency is muted by the absence of any measure of financial security. The National Association for the Visual Arts (NAVA) was one of two main dissenting voices to the National Cultural Policy.[46] At issue was the failure of Creative Australia to address non-payment of artists for their work. Seeking to redress this by advocating a $3 million-a-year contribution to underfunded galleries, they were disappointed.[47] More telling was that the association tied this commitment to changes in the social security legislation enabling artists to continue professional arts activities whilst drawing social security benefits. This approach resonates with the Belgian and French models and echoes with values in place in Ireland, Denmark, and until recently, New Zealand. Such changes to social security legislation would have a profound effect on artists' lives. It would fundamentally change the conditions that govern their daily life, making them more independent of the exigencies of policy shifts and changes of government.

Within the arts industry, the solution is increased levels of funding and so becomes a problem for government. But the industry has been complicit in growing the massive financial inequity that now exists between artists and non-artists. While freelance artists draw on average $7,000 a year from their practice, arts administrators command salaries upwards of $60,000 a year. Over the last fifteen years this inequity has increased and increasingly devastates the artists' ecology. It has been compounded by industry's acceptance of changes to funding allocations, poor advocacy and over-professionalisation.

A compelling example lies in the Arts Development category of Arts Victoria, the state's body which advises on and implements arts policy.[48] The Arts Development Program has been the primary source of support for Victoria's independent artists. In 1998 an eligible artist or company was able to apply for a presentation grant under Arts Development for up to $50,000. Applying CPI at published rates from 1998–2009,[49] the $50,000 in 1998 is equivalent to $70,400 in 2009–10. In 2010, grants for presentation were set at $30,000. This represents a drop of over $40,000 in real terms per grant. For the independent artist this is devastating because around two-thirds of these production grants are allocated to artists' fees. Indeed, production grants carried the expectation that 70% of the funding be so attributed. On that basis this represents a drop of $28,000 (from $49,000 to $21,000) of available artists' fees per production grant. In real terms and in this category's context, Victorian artists were worse off in 2009 by almost 60% than ten years previously, a dire situation made worse by the fact that the Victoria Commissions program that had provided $450,000 a year for new works to independent artists since 1994 was discontinued in 2003.

Of note, over a similar period Arts Victoria staffing levels generated new ceilings. In 1998 they were capped at 46. By 2009 there were reportedly 85 Arts Victoria full-time staff.[50] So over a period when the major source of Victorian artists' fees more than halved, Arts Victoria's staff budget almost doubled.

A local antidote to this sad state of affairs can be found in the thinking behind the document *Foundation for the Artist*.[51] The rhetoric, ideas and values underpinning this proposed entity coalesce the better current ideas on how to value the artist. It's a pretty straightforward gambit: pay them. So the key platform is financial, and a dizzying array of funding models is offered by its authors. Given the recent reforms it is unlikely that such a Foundation will get a guernsey, especially as the asking price for start-up is $15 million a year for three years. However, the tone and attitude of the language in the publication is promising as is the way in which research has been integrated into the fundamental ideas and strategies. It represents a significant appreciation of the value of the artist and a comprehensive articulation of the reasons behind it. Some of this has echoes in *Creative Australia*.

3

A necessary series of provocations

Here's the thing: Artists are not players. Our devaluation in the scheme of cultural things is the consequence of circumstances beyond our control. This is true. But artists have not only had their influence, income and autonomy reduced by these circumstances, *they have abnegated responsibility for adjusting to them*. One reason we no longer have a place at the table is that we gave it up. For example, amongst Victorian theatre artists more than ten years ago, an argument played out around the constant request to government for more funding to make our work. The prevailing view was that it was counter-productive to keep asking for more money because we never got it. The point, of course, was not *what* we were asking for but that we were asking. Our constant requests constituted visibility, presence and agitation. Since then, as other members of the arts industry have been advocating on our behalf, our visibility and agency in critical areas of policy have decreased. *By ceding advocacy for our cultural agency to non-artists, we have played ourselves out of the conversation. We are twice-removed from the power-spot.*

If over the last decade, Australians have lost their mojo, this is no less true of Australian artists. We have played a part in our own devaluation by allowing ourselves to be displaced from leadership, advisory and advocacy roles. Too often, articulate speeches in the comfort of the artists' community are heard nowhere else. Artists are fearful of speaking up for fear of retribution in the form of unsuccessful grant applications or upsetting the gatekeepers, whose support is essential to getting up projects, and of being categorised as 'difficult', 'opinionated', 'outspoken'. Whether true or not, it is an industry perception.[52] When independent artists step outside the confines of artistic practice and proffer opinions related to the broader issues of artistic and cultural production, they fear they may become easy targets because they have no group, company or organisation to protect them or their precarious livelihood. The paucity of input sought by media from independent artists on the national cultural policy indicates this process is self-perpetuating.

The reality is: we have nothing to lose. We have to put our hand up. Speak up. Refuse to back down for fear of retribution. Ask for more. When we don't get it, demand it. Prove we are the only essential element in the equation of artistic production. Challenge the industry and government to disprove it. Understand our social, cultural and economic value. Advocate for the arts as a public good. Don't get sucked into 'the market', 'the cultural product', the trade fair mentality. Arm ourselves with facts, figures, passion and rigour. Don't be dissuaded by small rewards. Persuade others of the benefits of putting artists smack-bang in the centre of every argument, contest, conflict and context in the process of artistic and cultural production. Do not remain silent.

In this spirit, here are a few provocations to assist:

Income

1: Advocacy for a Living Wage

This is a call on local, state and federal governments and their respective arts and cultural agencies and arms to commit to the advocacy of social security legislation that provides artists with a living wage in lieu of an unemployment benefit so that they may seek employment solely in their chosen profession and continue to develop their professional practice.

2: Salary Sacrifice

This is a call on local, state and federal governments to permit and enable the staff of their respective arts and cultural agencies and arms to commit to a salary sacrifice of 5% per annum to be placed in an Artists' Commission Pool, the funds of which are to be distributed annually for new work and subject to an assessment process undertaken with staff cooperation and input.

3. Influence

This is a call on local, state and federal governments and their respective arts and cultural agencies and arms to commit to 50% representation of professional artists on all assessment, consultative and governance panels (paid representation for those professional artists who identify as independent).

4. Agency

This is a call on local, state and federal governments to, in the case of the performing arts:

(a) distribute production funds directly to artists so that they can determine where they wish to present their work. This will enliven the sector by offsetting the institutionalisation of arts programming, increase the autonomy of artists and the flow of arts into the wider community.

(b) impose a five-year moratorium on all infrastructure and infrastructure-related grants. Funds set aside for these purposes are to be provided on five-year fellowships to develop artistic projects to which producers can apply for monies to support. This will ensure producing structures are created in response to artistic creation and not vice-versa.

National Artists' Strike

This is a call on all artists to undertake a rolling National Strike—a month-long retraction of the labour and goods of all artists including actors, dancers, musicians, choreographers, composers, designers, directors, sculptors, photographers, writers for theatre, film and television, media artists, digital artists, painters, sound artists.

All such artists in workplaces benefiting in any part from government subsidy, be it local, state or federal, are encouraged to cease work one day a week for the duration. Any artist whose work is performed or exhibited during this time is encouraged to withdraw that work for the duration. We sincerely regret the strike will cause the disruption or cancellation of theatre, dance, music and opera productions across the country as well as exhibitions of the visual arts in which the work of living artists is presented.

EPILOGUE

In 1983 I had dinner with George Harrison at Kinsella's in Sydney's Taylor Square. George spoke to everyone at the table driven by his innate curiosity about human beings. Our conversation turned to the then nuclear crisis which prompted him to offer that, if something went awry, Australia was his preferred destination. Around that time George purchased land on Hamilton Island and built a home there. Scroll forwards to present-day Australia, two years after Fukushima: the nuclear crisis is as real and forbidding now as it was then and Australia is still a viable escape clause for the rich and powerful should something 'go wrong'. The past tells us that we have learned nothing. We have trod water. Tadpoles in the pond.

Scroll forwards thirty years from now to 2043. If the artist is living and working under the same conditions, we will have trod water once again. And lost a great opportunity. The twenty-first century is our time: when what we do, what we make and how we work can have the greatest social benefit. We need to work through the ambient fear created by neo-liberalism, push back against the shadow values of managerialism and constitute ourselves as a sustained contradiction. To do this we must fight for fundamentals—industry representation, professional autonomy and financial security. From such a position we will be visible, capable and central to the key conversations about the arts in society, and help create a society with the arts at its centre. This is our future, the future we need for ourselves, for our children, for our culture and for our society.

If we have to take direct action to make that happen, so be it. We will be following in the footseps of nurses, teachers, miners, doctors, all who value their work and all whose work is valued. Until we appreciate the essential value of the artist in the New World Order, no one else will. We can no longer stay in the pond. We have to swim in the ocean. If we do, then the world will change for the better. Our capacity to shape and imagine a better future is necessary and real.

World Leaders Summit, Darwin, 2043

Prime Minister Jack Khan Shmik pondered the options. He was about to give the opening address to the World Leaders Summit and he wanted to hit the right note, to say something that would shape the proceedings of the next three days. His mind was a tumble-dryer, sorting items that needed more attention than others, all of them rolling around in a contained space. He mentally interrupted the cycle, opened the door and scrutinised the contents. A few things stood out. Colour, structure and form. Unsurprisingly, given his previous occupation as a painter—a highly collectable one, as his wife reminded him whenever she tried to dissuade him from seeking another term. How could he do that? He was as much a product of Australia's incredible success story as he was one of its architects. For thirty years he had watched and participated in the appreciation of the value of the artist, a process which had made his country the model for 'interconnectivity', the new mechanism-byword of the twenty-first century.

Artists had inserted themselves into every sticking-place of society, into the in-between spaces of the law, banking, manufacturing, environment, on the edges of everywhere and every thing. Their practices and processes, honed in the studio, the rehearsal room, in the privacy and safety of their minds, had become sought after as massive leaps in technology proposed problems that only an acute artistic sensibility could solve. Time and again, artists had developed better questions for solving difficult problems; time and again they had seen the connections between things when others could only see the 'things'; time and again artists had saved the world from seemingly imminent disaster by engaging the Artistic Mind, a new model for global progress that had been patented and exported to all corners of the world and had drawn its leaders to this city, one of its most remote. Australia was the Numbskull Nation no longer and today's opening address would mark an historical moment. He stood up still not knowing how to begin and then his mouth opened of its own volition, speaking the words that had become a mantra for a generation of global citizens: 'Long Live the Artist...'

Endnotes

1 Norman Fairclough, 'Critical discourse analysis in researching language in the new capitalism: overdetermination, transdisciplinary and textual analysis' in Claire Harrison and Lyn Young (eds.) *Systemic linguistics and critical discourse analysis*. London and New York: Continuum, p.103.

2 *Dutch News*.nl http://www.dutchnews.nl/news/archives/2011/11/culture_cuts_start_next_year.php.

3 *Fillip*, http://fillip.ca/content/responses-to-recent-dutch-arts-cuts/.

4 From September 2009–November 2011, David Pledger was the Inaugural director of the IETM-Australia Council Collaboration Project for which he was based in Brussels January 2010–August 2011.

5 Tobias Kokkelmans, A Line in The Sand', *Theater Schrift Lucifer* 10, Autumn 2010.

6 Adam Smith, *An Inquiry into the Nature and Causes of the Wealth of Nations*, Book 1, p.86, 'A plentiful subsistence increases the bodily strength of the labourer, and the comfortable hope of bettering his condition, and of ending his days perhaps in ease and plenty, animates him to exert that strength to the utmost.'

7 7. John Ralston Saul, *Dark Diversions*, Melbourne: Penguin (2012), Page 178. The protagonist, a writer, attends a lecture by noted Italian Fascist Gianfranco Fini of whom he observes: 'He was sewing together into one the original fascist corporatism with contemporary managerialism and the rising forces of neo-conservatism.'

8 Tobias Kokkelmans, 2010.

9 Nichole Georgeou and Susan Engel 'The Impact of Neoliberalism and New Managerialism on Development

Volunteering: An Australian Case Study', *Australian Journal of Political Science*, Melbourne: Deakin University 46:2, 2011, 297–311.

10 Hoopes, James. 'Managerialism: Its History and Dangers'. Boston: *Historically Speaking*, Journal of the Historical Society, University of Boston, Vol. 5 no.1 September 2003.

11 Nichole Georgeou and Susan Engel, 2011.

12 12. Patrick Fitzsimons, Managerialism and Education, *Encyclopaedia of Philosophy of Education*, 1999, p.5. http://www.ffst.hr/ENCYCLOPAEDIA/doku.php?id%20=%20managerialism_and_education&s[]fitzsimons.

13 Fitzsimons, 1999, p.4.

14 Kathy Keele was CEO of the Australia Council 2007–12. Her previous positions included Head of International Marketing and Product Development (BHP) and Managing Director (Telstra Mobile).

15 http://www.australiacouncil.gov.au/about/corporate_information.

16 http://www.australiacouncil.gov.au/about/corporate_information.

17 Fitzsimons, 1999, p.4.

18 *Artist Careers Research*, August 2010, Australia Council for the Arts http://www.australiacouncil.gov.au/resources/reports_and_publications/subjects/artists/artist_careers

19 See *Artist Careers Research* August 2010: 'What is your other job? the census study', p.14. Artist occupations' share of arts employment has progressively fallen from 35% in 1996 to 27% in 2006 while arts-related occupations' share has increased from 48% to 61% respectively.

20 Willard F. Enteman, *Managerialism : the emergence of a new ideology*. Madison, Wisconsin: University of Wisconsin, 1993

21 Production grants 'support the premiere season of public performances of a new work and the stages leading up to it, where a presenting partner has already

committed to a project. http://www.australiacouncil.gov.au/grants/2013/theatre-new-work

22 Carrillo Gantner, *Building Cultural Relations*. Canberra: ANU, Australian Centre on China In the World, 2013, p.2.

23 This survey was conducted in February 2013.

24 Sectoral Advisory Panels are the new mechanism for the provision of advice to the Governing Board. *Creative Australia: National Cultural Policy*, p.140. http://creativeaustralia.arts.gov.au/assets/Creative-Australia-PDF-20130417.pdf /

25 Peter Shergold, *New Models, New Money: Foundation for The Artist*. Discussion paper, Arts Queensland and Centre for Social Impact, UNSW, 2011.

26 David Throsby, and Anita Zednik, *Do you really expect to get paid? An Economic Study of Professional Artists in Australia*. Australian Council for the Arts 2010.

27 Juan Davila, 'Artist's statement' in ARC/Musée d'Art Moderne de la Ville de Paris, *D'un autre continent: L'Australie le rève et le réel*, exhibition catalogue, Paris 1983, p.102 as quoted in Chris McAuliffe,' Living the Dream', *Meanjin* 3, 2012 p.63.

28 Alison Carroll and Carrillo Gantner, *Finding a Place on the Asian Stage*, Sydney: Currency House, Platform Paper 31, 2012.

29 http://en.wikipedia.org/wiki/1997_Asian_financial_crisis.

30 http://www.cct.go.kr/english/hcac/vision.jsp.

31 http://vti.be/en/over-vti/mission.

32 http://en.wikipedia.org/wiki/List_of_countries_by_GDP_%28nominal%29.

33 *Sustainability Australia Report*, National Sustainability Council 2013, Section 15, Economic Indicators. http://www.environment.gov.au/sustainability/measuring/publications/sustainable-australia-report-2013.html

34 *Liveability Ranking and Overview*. London: The Economist Intelligence Unit, 2012.

35 In Conversation with Catarina Saraiva, Panorama Festival, Argentina, 2012.

36 Deleuze, Gilles and Félix Guattari. 1980. *A Thousand Plateaus*. Trans. Brian Massumi. London and New York: Continuum, 2004.

37 www.artdaily.org/index.asp?int_sec=2&int_new=60265#.UWVNQ4J0dfX (AFP).

38 http://www.goethe.de/uun/org/ltb/enindex.htm.

39 In the forum, *Asia + Europe = Australia Forum* at Arts House, Melbourne 2012, the EU Ambassador to Australia, David Daly, elegantly outlined our 'great Australian qualities', and then asked in the context of our dealing in Asia: 'do these qualities get in the way of listening?'

40 http://www.wearemore.eu/about/.

41 http://www.asoulforeurope.eu/about-us/mission-statement.

42 http://ec.europa.eu/education/lifelong-learning-programme/erasmus_en.htm.

43 http://www.guardian.co.uk/culture/2010/jan/24/artists-day-jobs.

44 http://eipcp.net/policies/2015/jacquemin/en.

45 Richard Flanagan, 'The Gambler'. Melbourne: *The Monthly*, February 2013.

46 Disability-in-the-arts advocacy groups, objected to offending language in the original document which was immediately changed.

47 http://www.visualarts.net.au/newsdesk/2013/03/nava-responds-to-ncpaus.

48 The Arts Development program supports Victoria's independent professional artists and arts organisations by enabling creative ideas to be realised, artistic and art-making practices to be strengthened, and artist's careers to be developed and sustained. In 2013 this program will be folded into a larger suite of grants programs called VicArts grants. http://www.arts. vic. gov.au/Funding_Programs/Arts_Development.

49 Australian Bureau of Statistics.

50 Arts Victoria's actual staff numbers are difficult to ascertain as they are buried within the Department of Premier and Cabinet staff numbers in its Annual Report. However in a document published by NEC in 2009 Arts Vic levels were published at 85 full-time staff. http://www.nec.com.au/media/docs/NEC%20Case%20Study_Arts%20Victoria-fde6292d 3184 412e-a5fd-101deb0bc05d-0.pdf

51 Throsby, and Zednik, 2010.

52 Tabrett, Leigh, *It's Culture, Stupid!* Reflections of an arts bureaucrat. Sydney: Currency House, Platform Papers 34, 2013.

Readers' Forum

A response to Jon Rose's *The Music of Place: Reclaiming the practice* (Platform Papers 35).

DR ALAN CADELL is a violinist and live music activist based at the Queensland Conservatorium where he completed his PhD in modern violin performance practices.

The Music of Place proposes a profoundly inspiring task for the twenty-first century Australian musician, that of 'reclaiming a practice', as Rose so eloquently puts it in his subtitle. The idea that Australia had the chance to make a truly ethnic musical practice all her own—much like America or Jamaica or other post-colonial nations—but, to put it in the vernacular, cocked it up, is truly compelling. Rose's proposition brings to mind the work of other radical violinists such as Tony Conrad and Henry Flynt, both of whom have also written deep tracts, sometimes laced with intense vitriol, about the path that European and American music took. What if Europeans chose Biber over Bach? What if Americans got infected with Bo Diddley fever instead of Beatle fever?

The history of Western music is full of these unfulfilled possibilities and Australia is clearly no different to the rest. Australian indigenous music history is appallingly overlooked, much like the poverty and desperation of some indigenous communities. Likewise our colonial and convict music history is still festering in an open wound that's unfortunately infected with the gangrene of nationalist morons giving it that racist undertone that other cultures have managed to push through and get past. In order to radicalise and transform a tradition, we have to face it and kick it in the teeth first. Like so much in Australian history, there is a shuddering sense of injustice pervading it all. Those of us who are descendants of nineteenth-century British migrants feel all too keenly the pain of our forefathers' mistakes and misdeeds, and what a way to heal them! Reclaiming a practice sounds to me like it could also help reclaim kinship—between indigenous and non-indigenous Australians—a shared history that is painful but shared nonetheless. That is, if it's done properly. Like other post-colonial nations we should be wary of repeating mistakes (and Rose does make poignant mention of the jindyworobakism for which many of our so-called great artists are responsible) and search for a cohesively mutual, diverse and heterogeneous culture that is free of the exploitation inherent, most particularly, in the history of post-war Western popular music. Keith Richards probably bought his first yacht while Chuck Berry rotted in jail, penniless.

As a musician who is, for better or worse, Australian, I feel charged with a desire to do something to help create the sort of utopia Rose proposes. I see *The Music of Place* as a Coo-ee to all musicians to reclaim the importance of music in our lives and, through this, to ultimately assist in making a better world. Like all utopias it is likely to fail, but it's definitely worth trying. We must reclaim the rightful place of musical practice—that is, an intense meaningful expression of a people intensely involved in the praxis of their own culture, thus bringing the necessary meaning and healing to whatever place it is they inhabit. We all have blood on our hands, and perhaps with Rose's music of place we could finally wash some of it off.

FORTHCOMING

PP37: November 2013

NOT AT A CINEMA NEAR YOU: AUSTRALIA'S FILM DISTRIBUTION PROBLEM

Lauren Carroll Harris

Does Australian really need better writers and directors to compete? Or should we first take a look at our film distribution?

Film is in flux. Theatrical releases are no longer working for local films. Only one in ten movie viewings occur at the cinema. Audience behaviour is changing.

Ancillary markets are no longer ancillary, they're *the* markets. This Platform Paper looks for solutions in a whole new environment. The mainstream Australian film industry and its policy makers are clinging to outmoded practices, Lauren Carroll Harris asserts. For too long they have reduced the 'film industry' to the 'production sector' and ignored the key factors for success: marketing, distribution and exhibition. Effective distribution and marketing have become more difficult than raising finance and producing. Harris examines the brightest examples of those filmmakers working with peer-to-peer, crowdfunded, low-cost and direct-to-viewer delivery, and poses the question: what can digital distribution do for Australian film? The answers are surprising and controversial.

Lauren Carroll Harris is a writer and artist whose film and arts writing appears regularly in *RealTime*, *The Sydney Morning Herald* and on radio. She is currently working on a PhD on film distribution in Australia.

AT YOUR LOCAL BOOKSHOP FROM 1 AUGUST
AND AS A PAPERBACK OR ELECTRONICALLY
FROM OUR WEBSITE AT
WWW.CURRENCYHOUSE.ORG.AU